You Know You're Drinking Too Much Coffee When . . .

You Know You're Drinking Too Much Coffee When . . .

AVIV M. ILAN & DAVID ILAN

ADAMS MEDIA CORPORATION
HOLBROOK, MASSACHUSETTS

Published by Adams Media Corporation
260 Center Street, Holbrook, MA 02343

ISBN: 1-55850-688-8

Printed in Canada.

J I H G F E D C B A

Library of Congress Cataloging-in-Publication Data
Ilan, Aviv M.
You know you're drinking too much coffee when— /
Aviv M. Ilan & David Ilan.
p.   cm.
ISBN 1-55850-688-8 (pb)
1. Coffee—Humor. I. Ilan, David. II. Title.
PN6231.C565I42   1996
818'.5403—dc20   96-28148
                                        CIP

Disclaimer: Any trademarks, advertising slogans, or colorful wide-brimmed
characters are the property of the company that owns them, and we make
no claims to ownership or to having originated them. This book should not
be used as a substitute for regular medical or psychological care in the treat-
ment of a coffee dependency. Also, we do not recommend using this book
as a coaster, oven mitt, or flotation device. Harmful if swallowed.

This book is available at quantity discounts for bulk purchases.
For information, call 1-800-872-5627
(in Massachusetts, 617-767-8100).

Visit our home page at http://www.adamsmedia.com

Dedication

To our three favorite things in life
—Daniel, Michal, and Avital

Acknowledgments

We would like to thank the following people for their invaluable help. Our friends and family, who for all intents and purposes, are one and the same: JACOB and HAVA ILAN, AMI IODER, AMY PREDMORE, and JERRY BIEDERMAN.

We would also like to thank our agent SHEREE BYKOFSKY, and ED WALTERS at ADAMS MEDIA CORPORATION, for their tremendous help and support with this book.

Introduction

Coffee plays many invaluable roles in our society. It helps millions of us wake up in the morning and keeps us perky throughout our daily routine. It brings us all closer together as we share our intimate thoughts, discuss politics, and recap the events of the day. It stirs up our passions for the finer things in life—art, music, poetry—and it inspires us to live, laugh, and love.

But there is also a dark side to this percolated pleasure. Excessive coffee consumption can brew up a whole world of trouble. A few double cappuccinos—and you're whipped into a frenzy. You salivate at the sound of metal scraping against ceramic. Your coffee breaks grow longer and longer and your work suffers. You find yourself frantically searching for your next cup.

Only in the glamorous, make-believe world of Hollywood can this addiction go untreated. In the real world, the consequences are many and the damage is real. This helpful guide can help you find out if you or someone you know has a "Coffee Condition." If so, please get help *instantly*. Realizing that you have a problem is half the solution, and this book is here to help.

**Juan Valdéz named his
donkey after you.**

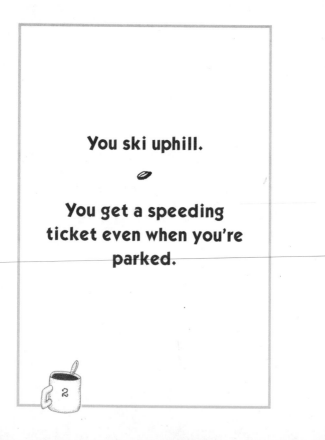

You ski uphill.

You get a speeding ticket even when you're parked.

2

You speed walk in your
sleep.

3

You have a bumper
sticker that says,
"Coffee drinkers are
good in the sack."

You answer the door
before people knock.

❁

You haven't blinked since
the last lunar eclipse.

You just completed another sweater and you don't know how to knit.

6

**You grind your coffee
beans in your mouth.**

7

Jai alai plays as slow as a
seniors' golf tournament
to you.

You have to watch videos in fast-forward.

You jump into a pool and
it starts to boil over.

You sleep with your eyes
open.

The only time you're standing still is during an earthquake.

You can take a picture of yourself from ten feet away without using the timer.

12

You lick your coffeepot clean.

You spend every vacation visiting "Maxwell House."

13

You listen to speed metal to relax.

You're the employee of the month at the local coffeehouse and you don't even work there.

15

**You've worn out your
third pair of tennis shoes
this week.**

**Your eyes stay open
when you sneeze.**

**You chew on other
people's fingernails.**

18

The nurse needs a
scientific calculator to
take your pulse.

**Your T-shirt says,
"Decaffeinated coffee is
the devil's coffee."**

You're so jittery that people use your hands to blend their margaritas.

You can type sixty words per minute with your feet.

22

You can jump-start your car without cables.

You have Styrofoam sofa covers.

24

If a kettle whistled in a forest, you'd hear it.

Cocaine is a downer.

**All your kids are named
"Joe."**

You don't need a hammer
to pound in nails.

**Your only source of
nutrition comes from
"Sweet & Low."**

28

You don't sweat, you percolate.

You buy milk by the barrel.

You've worn out the handle on your favorite mug.

You go to AA meetings just for the free coffee.

31

You walk twenty miles on
your treadmill before
you realize it's not
plugged in.

You forget to unwrap candy bars before eating them.

**Charles Manson thinks
you need to calm down.**

34

You've built a miniature city out of little plastic stirrers.

People get dizzy just watching you.

When you find a penny, you say, "Find a penny, pick it up. Sixty-three more, I'll have a cup."

You've worn the finish
off your coffee table.

**The Taster's Choice
couple wants to adopt
you.**

39

**Starbucks owns the
mortgage on your house.**

40

Your favorite snack is Styrofoam packing peanuts.

You've melted away your fillings.

42

Your taste buds are so numb you could drink your lava lamp.

You're so wired, you pick up AM radio.

People can test their batteries in your ears.

Your face is on a Colombian postage stamp.

Your life's goal is to amount to a hill of beans.

47

Lightning strikes you and _it_ gets perked up.

Your tongue has the words "Genuine Leather" stamped on it.

**Commodity traders use
you to predict the world
coffee market.**

Instant coffee takes too long.

**You channel surf faster
without the remote.**

When someone says,
"How are you?", you say,
"Good to the last drop."

You want to be cremated
just so you can spend the
rest of eternity in a
coffee can.

You want to come back
as a coffee mug in your
next life.

55

Your heartbeat sounds
like "rapa tapa tap tap . . .
ra tappa tap tap."

Your birthday is a national holiday in Brazil.

You'd be willing to spend
time in a Turkish prison.

You go to sleep just so
you can wake up and
smell the coffee.

You're offended when people use the word "brew" to mean beer.

People come to your house for poetry readings and open mike nights.

You name your cats "Cream" and "Sugar."

You get drunk just so you
can sober up.

You speak perfect
Arabic without ever
taking a lesson.

Your Thermos is on wheels.

Your lips are permanently stuck in the sipping position.

You have a picture of
your coffee mug on your
coffee mug.

67

You ride a stationary
bike to work.

68

You can outlast the
Energizer bunny.

You short out motion detectors.

You have a conniption
over spilled milk.

71

You have a bumper
sticker that says,
"Coffee drinkers stay up
all night."

72

You don't even wait for the water to boil anymore.

You melt the rink when you ice-skate.

You can play ping-pong without a partner.

Your nervous twitch registers on the Richter scale.

You list "coffee achiever" on your resume.

77

You think being called a
"drip" is a compliment.

78

You have a three-piece
suit made of burlap.

You smuggle coffee into
the country by burying it
in cocaine.

80

You can locate Angola on the map.

**Your blood type is
C8-H10-N4-O2.**

You have monogrammed coffee filters.

You drive around with a sign on your car that reads, "Caution: Driver under the influence of coffee."

84

You made provisions in your will for your coffee supply.

You took a full-time job just for the coffee breaks.

86

Your coffee mug has lip indentations on it.

You coined the phrase,
"A day without coffee is
like . . .
aaaaaauuuuugggghhhhh."

You tear open bean bags
just to make sure.

You use coffee-flavored mouthwash.

90

Your deep blue eyes are
now shallow brown.

You celebrate *every* moment of your life.

92

You pour mocha mix on
your cereal.

93

You have your mail
forwarded to a donut
shop.

🍩

You don't tan, you roast.

You constantly speak
like an auctioneer.

Your children don't come near you until you've had your first cup.

96

**The stewardess hands
you the whole pot.**

You have coffee stains on
your fingers.

Your teeth resemble
stalactites.

98

Everything you know you've learned from the backs of sugar packets.

99

You hold a seance to contact the spirit of coffee.

You measure your life in coffee spoons.

Your baby takes her milk steamed.

You meditate while listening to your "natural sounds of coffee brewing" CD.

Your motto is, "A cup a day keeps the doctor awake."

✐

You don't get mad, you get steamed.

The International Coffee Organization voted you "Drinker of the Year" again.

104

You have "his" and "hers"
coffeemakers.

You instinctively wake up one minute before your coffeemaker starts brewing to make sure it starts.

The Betty Ford Clinic opened a coffee ward just for you.

107

You had to remove your
car stereo to make room
for your cup holder.

If you had a nickel for every cup of coffee you drank . . . you'd buy more coffee.

109

Your three favorite
things in life are coffee
before and coffee after.

You carry a spare mug in your trunk.

When there's trouble brewing, you say, "I'll have a cup."

111

Your lover uses soft lights, romantic music, and a glass of iced coffee to get you in the mood.

You don't salivate, you foam.

Your personal ad reads,
"Coffee Lover ISOS. Must
have own mug. Send
photo of mug."

114

You belong to thirty-one "coffee-of-the-month" clubs so you'll never miss a day.

115

You can't even remember
your second cup.

❧

You help your dog chase
its tail.

You registered for your wedding at The Coffee Connection.

117

You championed 7/11's "It's fresh or it's free" policy.

You carry a portable, battery-operated coffee maker in your fanny pack.

119

**You insist on calling
every waiter "Jean-Luc."**

You soak your dentures
in coffee overnight.

❦

Dead Heads regard you
as a role model.

121

You think the "free refill"
is the greatest thing
since sliced bread.

122

Your kids sing, "I'm a little coffeepot, short and stout."

Your coffee mug is insured by Lloyds of London.

You have a pool in the shape of a coffee bean.

124

You introduce your
spouse as your
coffeemate.

125

You converted your car's radiator so you can brew up a pot while you drive.

126

Without you, the U.S. would not be the world's leading coffee consumer.

You think CPR stands for "Coffee Provides Resuscitation."

Your first-aid kit contains two pints of coffee with an I.V. hookup.

You think Folger's Crystals have healing powers.

You don't have body odor, you have a fine aroma.

Your breath wakes the dead.

131

**Your guidance counselor
has two words for you:
"bean counter."**

132

You have a bumper
sticker that says, "I
break for coffee."

❧

You don't mingle, you
blend.

133